The WORLD'S Greatest Collection of
QUOTES FOR

Dads

The WORLD'S Greatest Collection of
QUOTES FOR
Dads

BARBOUR
PUBLISHING

Published by Barbour Publishing, Inc., P.O. Box 719, Uhrichsville, Ohio 44683, www.barbourbooks.com

Our mission is to publish and distribute inspirational products offering exceptional value and biblical encouragement to the masses.

Member of the
Evangelical Christian
Publishers Association

Printed in the United States of America.

CONTENTS

PARENTHOOD

Parenthood: That state of being better chaperoned than you were before marriage.
MARCELENE COX

JESUS SAID. . ."COME TO ME, ALL YOU WHO ARE WEARY AND BURDENED, AND I WILL GIVE YOU REST."
MATTHEW 11:25, 28 NIV

We never know the love of our parents for us till we have become parents ourselves.
HENRY WARD BEECHER

It sometimes happens, even in the best of families, that a baby is born. This is not necessarily cause for alarm. The important thing is to keep your wits about you and borrow some money.
ELINOR GOULDING SMITH

People who say they sleep like
a baby usually don't have one.
LEO J. BURKE

THE TROUBLE WITH BEING A
PARENT IS THAT BY THE TIME
YOU ARE EXPERIENCED, YOU
ARE UNEMPLOYED.
AUTHOR UNKNOWN

We can't give our children the
future, strive though we may
to make it secure. But we can
give them the present.
KATHLEEN NORRIS

Parents: Persons who spend half
their time worrying how a child will
turn out and the rest of the time
wondering when a child will turn in.
TED COOK

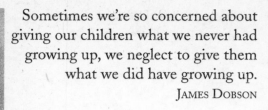

Sometimes we're so concerned about giving our children what we never had growing up, we neglect to give them what we did have growing up.
JAMES DOBSON

WHAT A CHILD DOESN'T RECEIVE HE CAN SELDOM LATER GIVE.
P. D. JAMES

Sometimes the poorest man leaves his children the richest inheritance.
RUTH E. RENKEL

Parents are often so busy with the physical rearing of children that they miss the glory of parenthood, just as the grandeur of the trees is lost when raking leaves.
MARCELENE COX

Every baby born into the world
is a finer one than the last.
CHARLES DICKENS

BABIES HAVE THE UNIQUE
ABILITY TO MAKE YOU
FEEL OLD WHILE
KEEPING YOU YOUNG.
BRUCE BICKEL AND STAN JANTZ

There are only two things a child
will share willingly—communicable
diseases and his mother's age.
BENJAMIN SPOCK

The voice of parents is the voice
of God's; for to their children,
they are heaven's lieutenants.
WILLIAM SHAKESPEARE

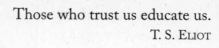

Those who trust us educate us.
T. S. ELIOT

The guys who fear becoming fathers don't understand that fathering is not something perfect men do, but something that perfects the man. The end product of child-raising is not the child but the parent.
FRANK PITTMAN

YOU KNOW YOU'RE A DAD WHEN YOU SAY THINGS LIKE. . . "AS LONG AS YOU LIVE UNDER MY ROOF, YOU'LL LIVE BY MY RULES."

You know you're a dad when you say things like. . . "I'm not just talking to hear my own voice!"

You know you're a dad
when you say things like. . .
"If your friend jumped
off a bridge, would you?"

YOU KNOW YOU'RE A
DAD WHEN YOU SAY
THINGS LIKE. . .
"IN MY DAY. . ."

You know you're a dad
when you say things like. . .
"Don't ask me; ask your mother."

Making the decision to have a
child is momentous. It is to decide
forever to have your heart go
walking around outside your body.
ELIZABETH STONE

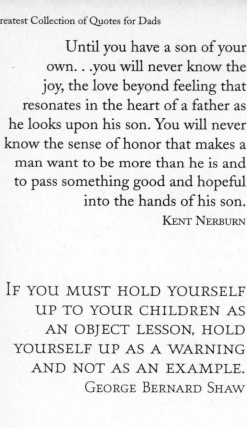

Until you have a son of your own. . .you will never know the joy, the love beyond feeling that resonates in the heart of a father as he looks upon his son. You will never know the sense of honor that makes a man want to be more than he is and to pass something good and hopeful into the hands of his son.

KENT NERBURN

IF YOU MUST HOLD YOURSELF UP TO YOUR CHILDREN AS AN OBJECT LESSON, HOLD YOURSELF UP AS A WARNING AND NOT AS AN EXAMPLE.

GEORGE BERNARD SHAW

There is no friendship, no love, like that of the parent for the child.

HENRY WARD BEECHER

There are only two things we should give our children. One is roots; the other, wings.
HODDING CARTER

MANY OF US HAVE INHERITED GREAT RICHES FROM OUR PARENTS—THE BANK ACCOUNT OF PERSONAL FAITH AND FAMILY PRAYERS.
NELS F. S. FERRE

In bringing up children, spend on them half as much money and twice as much time.
AUTHOR UNKNOWN

When you put faith, hope, and love together, you can raise positive kids in a negative world.
ZIG ZIGLAR

Noble fathers have
noble children.
EURIPIDES

CHILDREN ARE NATURAL
MIMICS WHO ACT LIKE THEIR
PARENTS, DESPITE EVERY
EFFORT TO TEACH THEM
GOOD MANNERS.
AUTHOR UNKNOWN

Human beings are the only creatures
on earth that allow their children
to come back home.
BILL COSBY

Before I got married, I had six theories
about bringing up children; now I have
six children and no theories.
JOHN WILMOT

I FELT SOMETHING IMPOSSIBLE FOR ME TO EXPLAIN IN WORDS. THEN, WHEN THEY TOOK HER AWAY, IT HIT ME. I GOT SCARED ALL OVER AGAIN AND BEGAN TO FEEL GIDDY. THEN IT CAME TO ME. . . . I WAS A FATHER.
NAT KING COLE

"Being a Father" is something mythical and infinitely important: a protector, who would keep a lid on all the chaotic and catastrophic possibilities of life.
TOM WOLFE

It is much easier to become a father than to be one.
KENT NERBURN

The beauty of "spacing" children many years apart lies in the fact that parents have time to learn the mistakes that were made with the older ones—which permits them to make exactly the opposite mistakes with the younger ones.

SYDNEY J. HARRIS

IT IS EASIER FOR A FATHER TO HAVE CHILDREN THAN FOR CHILDREN TO HAVE A REAL FATHER.

POPE JOHN XXIII

To a father growing old, nothing is dearer than a daughter.

EURIPIDES

No matter how calmly you try to referee, parenting will eventually produce bizarre behavior, and I'm not talking about the kids.

BILL COSBY

Now the thing about having a baby—and I can't be the first person to have noticed this—is that thereafter you have it.
JEAN KERR

IN THE FINAL ANALYSIS, IT IS NOT WHAT YOU DO FOR YOUR CHILDREN BUT WHAT YOU HAVE TAUGHT THEM TO DO FOR THEMSELVES THAT WILL MAKE THEM SUCCESSFUL HUMAN BEINGS.
ANN LANDERS

Nothing you do for children is ever wasted. They seem not to notice us, hovering, averting our eyes; and they seldom offer thanks, but what we do for them is never wasted.
GARRISON KEILLOR

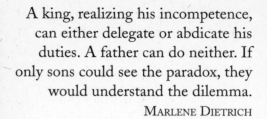

A king, realizing his incompetence, can either delegate or abdicate his duties. A father can do neither. If only sons could see the paradox, they would understand the dilemma.

MARLENE DIETRICH

IT KILLS YOU TO SEE THEM GROW UP. BUT I GUESS IT WOULD KILL YOU QUICKER IF THEY DIDN'T.

BARBARA KINGSOLVER

It would seem that something which means poverty, disorder, and violence every single day should be avoided entirely, but the desire to beget children is a natural urge.

PHYLLIS DILLER

Let parents bequeath to their children not riches, but the spirit of reverence.

PLATO

In America there are two classes of travel—first class, and with children.
ROBERT BENCHLEY

DON'T WORRY THAT CHILDREN NEVER LISTEN TO YOU; WORRY THAT THEY ARE ALWAYS WATCHING YOU.
ROBERT FULGHUM

Parents often talk about the younger generation as if they didn't have anything to do with it.
HAIM GINOTT

Give me the life of the boy whose mother is nurse, seamstress, washerwoman, cook, teacher, angel, and saint, all in one, and whose father is guide, exemplar, and friend. No servants to come between. These are the boys who are born to the best fortune.
ANDREW CARNEGIE

21

Fathers send their sons to college
either because they went
to college or they didn't.
L. L. HENDREN

HAVING CHILDREN MAKES
ONE NO MORE A PARENT
THAN HAVING A PIANO
MAKES YOU A PIANIST.
MICHAEL LEVINE

[Baby] was the tiniest thing I ever
decided to put my whole life into.
TERRI GUILLEMETS

FAMILY MATTERS

The happiest moments of my life have been the few which I have passed at home in the bosom of my family.
THOMAS JEFFERSON

AS ARROWS ARE IN THE HAND OF A MIGHTY MAN; SO ARE CHILDREN OF THE YOUTH. HAPPY IS THE MAN THAT HATH HIS QUIVER FULL OF THEM.
PSALM 127:4–5 KJV

Govern a family as you would cook a small fish—very gently.
CHINESE PROVERB

Family is the most important thing in the world.
PRINCESS DIANA

HAPPINESS IS TO BE
FOUND ONLY IN THE HOME
WHERE GOD IS LOVED AND
HONORED, WHERE EACH ONE
LOVES, AND HELPS, AND CARES
FOR THE OTHERS.
THÉOPHANE VÉNARD

The simple exercise of praying
together regularly as a family will do
more to strengthen your family than
anything else you could do together.
BRUCE BICKEL AND STAN JANTZ

For many people, the heavy
responsibilities of home and family
and earning a living absorb all their
time and strength. Yet such a home—
where love is—may be a light shining
in a dark place, a silent witness to the
reality and the love of God.
OLIVE WYON

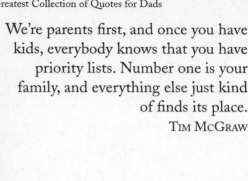

We're parents first, and once you have kids, everybody knows that you have priority lists. Number one is your family, and everything else just kind of finds its place.

TIM MCGRAW

THE BEST WAY TO KEEP CHILDREN AT HOME IS TO MAKE THE HOME ATMOSPHERE PLEASANT AND LET THE AIR OUT OF THE TIRES.

DOROTHY PARKER

We are always too busy for our children; we never give them the time or interest they deserve. We lavish gifts upon them; but the most precious gift, our personal association, which means so much to them, we give grudgingly.

MARK TWAIN

Bring love into your home, for
this is where our love for
each other must start.
MOTHER TERESA

PERHAPS THE GREATEST
SOCIAL SERVICE THAT
CAN BE RENDERED BY
ANYBODY TO THE COUNTRY
AND TO MANKIND IS TO
BRING UP A FAMILY.
GEORGE BERNARD SHAW

In some families, *please* is described
as the magic word. In our house,
however, it was *sorry*.
MARGARET LAURENCE

When a father gives to his son,
both laugh; when a son gives
to his father, both cry.
JEWISH PROVERB

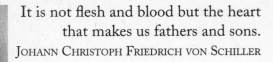

It is not flesh and blood but the heart
that makes us fathers and sons.
JOHANN CHRISTOPH FRIEDRICH VON SCHILLER

SACRED AND HAPPY HOMES
ARE THE SUREST GUARANTEES
FOR THE MORAL PROGRESS
OF A NATION.
HENRY DRUMMOND

The family: We were a strange
little band of characters trying
to figure out the common thread
that bound us all together.
ERMA BOMBECK

Having a family is like having a
bowling alley installed in your brain.
MARTIN MULL

No matter what you've done for yourself or for humanity, if you can't look back on having given love and attention to your own family, what have you really accomplished?
LEE IACOCCA

THE FAMILY IS THE NUCLEUS OF CIVILIZATION.
WILLIAM J. DURANT

The ideal home: big enough for you to hear the children, but not very well.
MIGNON MCLAUGHLIN

When I was a child, my family's menu consisted of two choices: take it or leave it.
BUDDY HACKETT

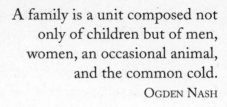

A family is a unit composed not
only of children but of men,
women, an occasional animal,
and the common cold.
OGDEN NASH

IF IT SEEM EVIL UNTO YOU TO
SERVE THE LORD, CHOOSE YOU
THIS DAY WHOM YE WILL
SERVE. . .BUT AS FOR
ME AND MY HOUSE,
WE WILL SERVE THE LORD.
JOSHUA 24:15 KJV

If the family were a fruit, it would
be an orange, a circle of sections
held together but separable—
each segment distinct.
LETTY COTTIN POGREBIN

Families are like fudge. . .mostly
sweet with a few nuts.
AUTHOR UNKNOWN

Good, honest, hardheaded character is a function of the home. If the proper seed is sown there and properly nourished for a few years, it will not be easy for that plant to be uprooted.
GEORGE A. DORSEY

EVERY CHRISTIAN FAMILY OUGHT TO BE, AS IT WERE, A LITTLE CHURCH CONSECRATED TO CHRIST AND WHOLLY INFLUENCED AND GOVERNED BY HIS RULES.
JONATHAN EDWARDS

To us, family means putting your arms around each other and being there.
BARBARA BUSH

Kids learn by example. If I respect Mom, they're going to respect Mom.
TIM ALLEN

Families with babies and
families without babies
are sorry for each other.
ED HOWE

WE CAN'T FORM OUR
CHILDREN ON OUR OWN
CONCEPTS; WE MUST TAKE
THEM AND LOVE THEM AS
GOD GIVES THEM TO US.
JOHANN WOLFGANG VON GOETHE

Our most basic instinct is not for
survival but for family. Most of
us would give our own life for the
survival of a family member, yet we
lead our daily life too often as if we
take our family for granted.
PAUL PEARSALL

TRIBUTE TO DAD

He that raises a large family does, indeed, while he lives to observe them, stand a broader mark for sorrow, but then he stands a broader mark for pleasure, too.

BENJAMIN FRANKLIN

ANY MAN CAN BE A FATHER, BUT IT TAKES A SPECIAL PERSON TO BE A DAD.

ANONYMOUS

There is no more vital calling or vocation for men than fathering.

JOHN THROOP

My dad told me when I went into high school, "It's not what you do when you walk in the door that matters. It's what you do when you walk out." That's when you've made a lasting impression.

JIM THOME

You know you're a dad when you say
things like. . .
"A little dirt never hurt anyone. . . .
Just wipe it off."

You know you're a
dad when you say
things like. . .
"I told you. . .keep your
eye on the ball."

You know you're a dad when you say
things like. . .
"We're not lost. I'm just not sure
where we are."

Sons are a heritage from the LORD,
children a reward from him.
PSALM 127:3 NIV

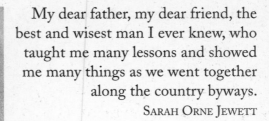

My dear father, my dear friend, the
best and wisest man I ever knew, who
taught me many lessons and showed
me many things as we went together
along the country byways.

SARAH ORNE JEWETT

LIFE AFFORDS NO GREATER
RESPONSIBILITY, NO GREATER
PRIVILEGE, THAN THE RAISING
OF THE NEXT GENERATION.

C. EVERETT KOOP

My dear father! When I remember
him, it is always with his arms open
wide to love and comfort me.

ISOBEL FIELD

A father carries pictures where
his money used to be.

AUTHOR UNKNOWN

Children are poor men's riches.
ENGLISH PROVERB

BLESSED INDEED IS THE MAN
WHO HEARS MANY GENTLE
VOICES CALL HIM *FATHER*!
LYDIA M. CHILD

F. . . You are my friend.
A. . . You are my ally.
T. . . You are my teacher.
H. . . You are my hero.
E. . . You are my example.
R. . . You are my rock.
K. WILLIAMS

None of the things I remember about
my father had anything at all to do
with his lifestyle or whom he knew or
the places he had been or the style of
the clothes he wore. I just knew that
he was always there.
CAL THOMAS

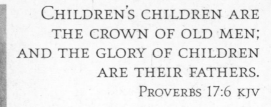

CHILDREN'S CHILDREN ARE
THE CROWN OF OLD MEN;
AND THE GLORY OF CHILDREN
ARE THEIR FATHERS.
PROVERBS 17:6 KJV

I watched a small man with
thick calluses on both hands work
fifteen and sixteen hours a day. I saw
him once literally bleed from the
bottoms of his feet, a man who came
here uneducated, alone, unable to
speak the language, who taught me all
I needed to know about faith and
hard work by the simple
eloquence of his example.
MARIO CUOMO

My father gave me the greatest gift
anyone could give another person—
he believed in me.
JIM VALVANO

One night a father overheard his son pray, "Dear God, make me the kind of man my daddy is."

Later that night, the father prayed, "Dear God, make me the kind of man my son wants me to be."
ANONYMOUS

MY HEROES ARE AND WERE MY PARENTS. I CAN'T SEE HAVING ANYONE ELSE AS MY HEROES.
MICHAEL JORDAN

People ask me if I ever see my father, and I say yes—because he puts in the effort. He calls all the time to tell us he's proud of us.
JENNA BUSH

The greatest gift I ever had came from God, and I call him Dad!
ANONYMOUS

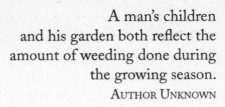

A man's children
and his garden both reflect the
amount of weeding done during
the growing season.
AUTHOR UNKNOWN

I HAVE NO GREATER JOY THAN
TO HEAR THAT MY CHILDREN
WALK IN TRUTH.
3 JOHN 1:4 KJV

It's only when you grow up and
step back from him, or leave him
for your own career and your own
home—it's only then that you can
measure his greatness and fully
appreciate it. Pride reinforces love.
MARGARET TRUMAN

Every man is rich who has
a child to love and guide.
OUR DAILY BREAD

Father!—to God Himself, we cannot give a holier name.
WILLIAM WORDSWORTH

I'VE HAD A HARD LIFE, BUT MY HARDSHIPS ARE NOTHING AGAINST THE HARDSHIPS THAT MY FATHER WENT THROUGH IN ORDER TO GET ME TO WHERE I STARTED.
BARTRAND HUBBARD

He didn't tell me how to live; he lived, and let me watch him do it.
CLARENCE BUDINGTON KELLAND

I talk and talk and talk, and I haven't taught people in fifty years what my father taught by example in one week.
MARIO CUOMO

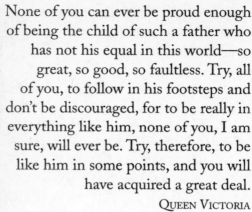

None of you can ever be proud enough of being the child of such a father who has not his equal in this world—so great, so good, so faultless. Try, all of you, to follow in his footsteps and don't be discouraged, for to be really in everything like him, none of you, I am sure, will ever be. Try, therefore, to be like him in some points, and you will have acquired a great deal.

QUEEN VICTORIA

I LOVE MY FATHER AS THE STARS—HE'S A BRIGHT, SHINING EXAMPLE AND A HAPPY TWINKLING IN MY HEART.

ADABELLA RADICI

When you teach your son, you teach your son's son.

THE TALMUD

A FATHER'S WISDOM

He who teaches children
learns more than they do.
GERMAN PROVERB

DURING THE COURSE OF
THE DAY, I FREQUENTLY
ASK THE LORD TO GIVE
ME WISDOM TO USE THE
KNOWLEDGE THAT I HAVE
AND TO GIVE ME PERSPECTIVE
AND UNDERSTANDING,
PARTICULARLY WHEN
DIFFICULT SITUATIONS ARISE.
BEN CARSON

Train up a child in the way he
should go: and when he is old,
he will not depart from it.
PROVERBS 22:6 KJV

We cannot always build the
future for our youth, but we can
build our youth for the future.
FRANKLIN D. ROOSEVELT

Live so that when your children
think of fairness and integrity,
they think of you.
H. JACKSON BROWN

THERE'S NOTHING THAT CAN
HELP YOU UNDERSTAND YOUR
BELIEFS MORE THAN TRYING
TO EXPLAIN THEM TO AN
INQUISITIVE CHILD.
FRANK A. CLARK

My son, despise not the chastening
of the LORD; neither be weary of
his correction: For whom the LORD
loveth he correcteth; even as a father
the son in whom he delighteth.
PROVERBS 3:11–12 KJV

Discipline doesn't break a child's
spirit half as often as the lack of
it breaks a parent's heart.
ANONYMOUS

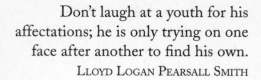

Don't laugh at a youth for his affectations; he is only trying on one face after another to find his own.
LLOYD LOGAN PEARSALL SMITH

A PARENT MUST RESPECT THE SPIRITUAL PERSON OF HIS CHILD AND APPROACH IT WITH REVERENCE.
GEORGE MACDONALD

"Hear, O Israel! The LORD is our God, the LORD alone. And you must love the LORD your God with all your heart, all your soul, and all your strength. And you must commit yourselves wholeheartedly to these commands I am giving you today. Repeat them again and again to your children. Talk about them when you are at home and when you are away on a journey, when you are lying down and when you are getting up again."
DEUTERONOMY 6:4–7 NLT

It behooves a father to be blameless if
he expects his child to be.
HOMER

THERE IS ONLY ONE WAY TO
BRING UP A CHILD IN THE
WAY HE SHOULD GO, AND
THAT IS TO TRAVEL THAT
WAY YOURSELF.
ABRAHAM LINCOLN

Character is largely caught, and the
father and the home should be the
great sources of character infection.
FRANK H. CHELEY

To be in your children's memories
tomorrow, you have to be
in their lives today.
ANONYMOUS

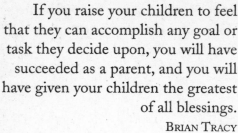

If you raise your children to feel that they can accomplish any goal or task they decide upon, you will have succeeded as a parent, and you will have given your children the greatest of all blessings.

BRIAN TRACY

EDUCATE YOUR CHILDREN TO SELF-CONTROL, TO THE HABIT OF HOLDING PASSION AND PREJUDICE AND EVIL TENDENCIES SUBJECT TO AN UPRIGHT AND REASONING WILL, AND YOU HAVE DONE MUCH TO ABOLISH MISERY FROM THEIR FUTURE AND CRIMES FROM SOCIETY.

BENJAMIN FRANKLIN

The father of the righteous shall greatly rejoice: and he that begetteth a wise child shall have joy of him.

PROVERBS 23:24 KJV

You have a lifetime to work, but children are only young once.
POLISH PROVERB

PROPERTY LEFT TO A CHILD MAY SOON BE LOST; BUT THE INHERITANCE OF VIRTUE—A GOOD NAME, AN UNBLEMISHED REPUTATION—WILL ABIDE FOREVER. IF THOSE WHO ARE TOILING FOR WEALTH TO LEAVE THEIR CHILDREN WOULD BUT TAKE HALF THE PAINS TO SECURE FOR THEM VIRTUOUS HABITS, HOW MUCH MORE SERVICEABLE WOULD THEY BE. THE LARGEST PROPERTY MAY BE WRESTED FROM A CHILD, BUT VIRTUE WILL STAND BY HIM TO THE LAST.
WILLIAM GRAHAM SUMNER

A soft answer turneth away wrath: but grievous words stir up anger.
PROVERBS 15:1 KJV

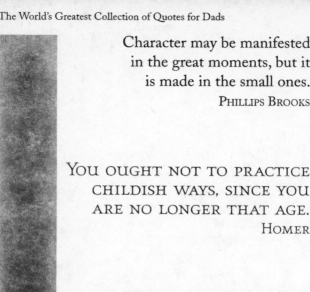

Character may be manifested
in the great moments, but it
is made in the small ones.
PHILLIPS BROOKS

YOU OUGHT NOT TO PRACTICE
CHILDISH WAYS, SINCE YOU
ARE NO LONGER THAT AGE.
HOMER

We have a suggestion for the
perfect gift for your child.
It is not easy to find, and it
is terribly expensive; but we
guarantee that it will last a lifetime,
and it will be your child's favorite.
We're talking about your *time*.
BRUCE BICKEL AND STAN JANTZ

The just man walketh in his integrity:
his children are blessed after him.
PROVERBS 20:7 KJV

It is a wise father that
knows his own child.
WILLIAM SHAKESPEARE

AS A FATHER HAS COMPASSION
ON HIS CHILDREN, SO THE
LORD HAS COMPASSION ON
THOSE WHO FEAR HIM.
PSALM 103:13 NIV

Few things help an individual
more than to place responsibility
upon him and to let him know
that you trust him.
BOOKER T. WASHINGTON

The best portion of a good man's life
is his little, nameless, unremembered
acts of kindness and love.
WILLIAM WORDSWORTH

"Wherever your treasure is, there your heart and thoughts will also be."
MATTHEW 6:21 NLT

DON'T BE MISLED BY THE MYTH OF "QUALITY TIME"— IT IS AN ADMIRABLE GOAL, BUT IT SHOULD NOT BE USED AS AN EXCUSE FOR MISSING "QUANTITY TIME" WITH YOUR CHILD. QUALITY MOMENTS USUALLY CANNOT BE SCHEDULED. THEY HAPPEN SPONTANEOUSLY, WITHOUT WARNING, IN CIRCUMSTANCES YOU DON'T ANTICIPATE.
BRUCE BICKEL AND STAN JANTZ

Watch yourselves closely so that you do not forget the things your eyes have seen or let them slip from your heart as long as you live. Teach them to your children and to their children after them.
DEUTERONOMY 4:9 NIV

Pray that you may be an example
and a blessing unto others and
that you may live more to the
glory of your Master.

CHARLES H. SPURGEON

THE GOD WHO MADE YOUR
CHILDREN WILL HEAR YOUR
PETITIONS. AFTER ALL,
HE LOVES THEM MORE
THAN YOU DO.

JAMES DOBSON

Is prayer your steering
wheel or your spare tire?

CORRIE TEN BOOM

Fathers, do not exasperate your
children; instead, bring them up
in the training and instruction
of the Lord.

EPHESIANS 6:4 NIV

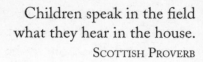

Children speak in the field
what they hear in the house.
SCOTTISH PROVERB

LIKE ALL MORAL VALUES,
RESPECT IS CAUGHT MORE
THAN IT IS TAUGHT.
BRUCE BICKEL AND STAN JANTZ

If you want children to keep their
feet on the ground, put some
responsibility on their shoulders.
ABIGAIL VAN BUREN

If you want your children to improve,
let them overhear the nice things you
say about them to others.
HAIM GINOTT

Children are apt to live up
to what you believe of them.
LADY BIRD JOHNSON

Too many of today's children have straight teeth and crooked morals.
UNKNOWN HIGH SCHOOL PRINCIPAL

DO NOT CONFINE YOUR CHILDREN TO YOUR OWN LEARNING, FOR THEY WERE BORN IN ANOTHER TIME.
HEBREW PROVERB

By profession I am a soldier and take pride in that fact. But I am prouder—infinitely prouder—to be a father. A soldier destroys in order to build; the father only builds, never destroys. The one has the potentiality of death; the other embodies creation and life. And while the hordes of death are mighty, the battalions of life are mightier still. It is my hope that my son, when I am gone, will remember me not from the battlefield but in the home repeating with him our simple daily prayer, "Our Father who art in heaven."
DOUGLAS MACARTHUR

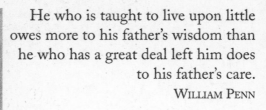

He who is taught to live upon little owes more to his father's wisdom than he who has a great deal left him does to his father's care.

WILLIAM PENN

BEAR IN MIND THAT THE WONDERFUL THINGS YOU LEARN IN YOUR SCHOOLS ARE THE WORK OF MANY GENERATIONS. ALL THIS IS PUT IN YOUR HANDS AS YOUR INHERITANCE IN ORDER THAT YOU MAY RECEIVE IT, HONOR IT, ADD TO IT, AND ONE DAY FAITHFULLY HAND IT ON TO YOUR CHILDREN.

ALBERT EINSTEIN

A truly rich man is one whose children run into his arms when his hands are empty.

AUTHOR UNKNOWN

The words a father speaks to his children in the privacy of the home are not overheard at the time, but as in whispering galleries, they will be clearly heard at the end and by posterity.

JEAN PAUL RICHTER

DON'T BE DISCOURAGED IF YOUR CHILDREN REJECT YOUR ADVICE. YEARS LATER, THEY WILL OFFER IT TO THEIR OWN OFFSPRING.

AUTHOR UNKNOWN

The hardest part of raising a child is teaching them to ride a bicycle. A shaky child on a bicycle for the first time needs both support and freedom. The realization that this is what the child will always need can hit hard.

SLOAN WILSON

You can learn many things from
children. How much patience
you have, for instance.

FRANKLIN P. JONES

WHAT OTHER NATION IS
SO GREAT AS TO HAVE THEIR
GODS NEAR THEM THE
WAY THE LORD OUR GOD
IS NEAR US WHENEVER WE
PRAY TO HIM?

DEUTERONOMY 4:7 NIV

Choose my instruction
rather than silver,
and knowledge rather
than pure gold.
For wisdom is far
more valuable than rubies.
Nothing you desire
can compare with it.

PROVERBS 8:10–11 NLT

A FATHER'S LOVE

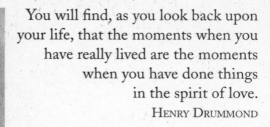

You will find, as you look back upon
your life, that the moments when you
have really lived are the moments
when you have done things
in the spirit of love.
HENRY DRUMMOND

LOVE GIVES ITSELF;
IT IS NOT BOUGHT.
HENRY WADSWORTH LONGFELLOW

We find delight in the beauty and
happiness of children that makes the
heart too big for the body.
RALPH WALDO EMERSON

Bricks and mortar make a house,
but the laughter of children
makes a home.
IRISH PROVERB

LET US LOOK UPON OUR
CHILDREN, LET US LOVE
THEM AND TRAIN THEM, AS
CHILDREN OF THE COVENANT
AND CHILDREN OF THE
PROMISE—THESE
ARE THE CHILDREN OF GOD.
ANDREW MURRAY

As God's child, today is your best day
because you are totally and completely
dependent upon Him. . . . God is your
only rock, your only security, your
only certainty, and your only
hope. . . . Dependency upon God
means that your life is in the hands
of the One who created the heavens,
who designed the galaxies, who
painted the sunsets, who set the earth
in space, and whose hand formed
every creature that walks, swims,
crawls, runs, or flies. Dependency
upon God means that you have set
your heart upon Him and put your
faith in Him. God will not fail you.
ROY LESSIN

For God so loved the world,
that he gave his only begotten Son,
that whosoever believeth in him
should not perish, but have
everlasting life.
JOHN 3:16 KJV

A MAN NEVER STANDS AS
TALL AS WHEN HE KNEELS
TO HELP A CHILD.
KNIGHTS OF PYTHAGORAS

How many hopes and fears, how
many ardent wishes and anxious
apprehensions are twisted together
in the threads that connect the
parent with the child!
SAMUEL G. GOODRICH

A good father reflects
the love of the heavenly Father.
AUTHOR UNKNOWN

[God] made fathers to
stand by our side,
To inspire us in every endeavor,
Whose faith and devotion
will last through our lives
And whose love
we will cherish forever.
AUTHOR UNKNOWN

CAST ALL YOUR ANXIETY
ON HIM BECAUSE HE
CARES FOR YOU.
1 PETER 5:7 NIV

We are to love God whole-
heartedly and teach our children
to do the same. That's the kind of
legacy that will last for generations
and please God into eternity.
BRUCE BICKEL AND STAN JANTZ

LOVE IS AN IMAGE OF GOD.
MARTIN LUTHER

The love of God is greater far
Than tongue or pen can ever tell;
It goes beyond the highest star,
And reaches to the lowest hell.
The guilty pair,
bowed down with care,
God gave His Son to win;
His erring child He reconciled,
And pardoned from his sin.

O love of God, how rich and pure!
How measureless and strong!
It shall forever more endure
The saints' and angels' song.
FREDERICK MARTIN LEHMAN

You have to love your children
unselfishly. That is hard.
But it is the only way.
BARBARA BUSH

BELOVED, LET US LOVE ONE
ANOTHER: FOR LOVE IS OF
GOD; AND EVERY ONE THAT
LOVETH IS BORN OF GOD,
AND KNOWETH GOD.
1 JOHN 4:7 KJV

"I am learning never to be
disappointed, but to praise," Arnot
of Central Africa wrote in his journal
long ago. . . . I think it must hurt the
tender love of our Father when we
press for reasons for His dealings with
us, as though He were not Love, as
though not He but another chose our
inheritance for us, and as though what
He chose to allow could be less than
the very best and dearest that Love
Eternal had to give.
AMY CARMICHAEL

Be kind to thy father; for when thou were young, who loved thee so fondly as he? He caught the first accents that fell from thy tongue and joined in thy innocent glee.

MARGARET COURTNEY

A DAUGHTER IS A GIFT OF LOVE.

AUTHOR UNKNOWN

Small boys become big men through the influence of big men who care about small boys.

ANONYMOUS

How strong and sweet my Father's care,
That round about me, like the air,
Is with me always, everywhere!
He cares for me!

JAMES R. MURRAY

Talk not of wasted affection;
affection never was wasted.
HENRY WADSWORTH LONGFELLOW

ALL LOVE IS SWEET,
GIVEN OR RETURNED.
PERCY BYSSHE SHELLEY

There are two great injustices that can
befall a child. One is to punish him
for something he didn't do. The other
is to let him get away with doing
something he knows is wrong.
ROBERT GARDNER

A father to the fatherless, a
defender of widows, is God
in his holy dwelling.
PSALM 68:5 NIV

Certain is it that there is no kind of
affection so purely angelic as of a
father to a daughter. In love to our
wives, there is desire; to our sons,
ambition; but to our daughters, there
is something which there are
no words to express.

JOSEPH ADDISON

Wide, wide as the ocean,
High as the Heaven above;
Deep, deep as the deepest sea
Is my Savior's love.
I, though so unworthy,
Still am a child of His care;
For His Word teaches me
That His love reaches
me everywhere.

CHARLES AUSTIN MILES

One may give without loving,
but one cannot love without giving.

AUTHOR UNKNOWN

You know. . .fathers just have a
way of putting everything together.
ERIKA COSBY

NOT FATHER OR MOTHER
HAS LOVED YOU AS GOD
HAS, FOR IT WAS THAT YOU
MIGHT BE HAPPY HE GAVE
HIS ONLY SON.
HENRY WADSWORTH LONGFELLOW

How great is the love the Father
has lavished on us, that we should
be called children of God! And
that is what we are!
1 JOHN 3:1 NIV

Behold th' amazing gift of love
The Father hath bestowed
On us, the sinful sons of men,
To call us sons of God!
ISAAC WATTS

To her, the name of *Father* was
another name for *love*.
FANNY FERN

LOVE AND FEAR: EVERYTHING
THE FATHER OF A FAMILY
SAYS MUST INSPIRE ONE
OR THE OTHER.
JOSEPH JOUBERT

Never forget that the most
powerful force on earth is love.
NELSON ROCKEFELLER

Our goal is to steadily turn our
children away from their earthly
parents, who will let them down,
toward a heavenly Father who will
always be there for them and in whose
arms they will always be secure.
SUSAN ALEXANDER YATES

"I will be a Father to you, and you
shall be My sons and daughters,
says the LORD Almighty."
2 CORINTHIANS 6:18 NKJV

TO BE ABLE TO SAY
HOW MUCH YOU LOVE
IS TO LOVE BUT LITTLE.
FRANCESCO PETRARCH

I love these little ones, and it is not
a slight thing when they, who are so
fresh from God, love us.
CHARLES DICKENS

Love and a cough cannot be hid.
GEORGE HERBERT

A daughter may outgrow your lap, but
she will never outgrow your heart.
AUTHOR UNKNOWN

Mother Nature is providential. She gives us twelve years to develop a love for our children before turning them into teenagers.

WILLIAM GALVIN

Behold, what love, what boundless love,
The Father hath bestowed
On sinners lost, that we should be
Now called "the sons of God"!

No longer far from Him but now
By "precious blood" made nigh,
Accepted in the "Well beloved,"
Near to God's heart we lie.

Behold, what manner of love!
What manner of love the Father
hath bestowed upon us,
That we, that we should be called,
Should be called the sons of God!

IRA D. SANKEY

A CHILDLIKE PERSPECTIVE

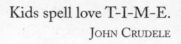

Kids spell love T-I-M-E.

JOHN CRUDELE

CHILDREN ARE BORN
TRUE SCIENTISTS. THEY
SPONTANEOUSLY EXPERIMENT
AND EXPERIENCE AND
REEXPERIENCE AGAIN. THEY
SELECT, COMBINE, AND TEST,
SEEKING TO FIND ORDER IN
THEIR EXPERIENCES—"WHICH
IS THE MOSTEST? WHICH IS
THE LEASTEST?" THEY SMELL,
TASTE, BITE, AND TOUCH-TEST
FOR HARDNESS, SOFTNESS,
SPRINGINESS, ROUGHNESS,
SMOOTHNESS, COLDNESS,
WARMNESS; THEY HEFT,
SHAKE, PUNCH, SQUEEZE,
PUSH, CRUSH, RUB, AND TRY
TO PULL THINGS APART.

R. BUCKMINSTER FULLER

One father is more than
a hundred schoolmasters.

GEORGE HERBERT

"Let the little children come to Me, and do not forbid them; for of such is the kingdom of heaven."
MATTHEW 19:14 NKJV

EVEN A CHILD IS KNOWN BY HIS DOINGS, WHETHER HIS WORK BE PURE, AND WHETHER IT BE RIGHT.
PROVERBS 20:11 KJV

Glory to the Father give,
God in whom we move and live;
Children's prayers He deigns to hear,
Children's songs delight His ear.
JAMES MONTGOMERY

A child's life is like a piece of paper on which every person leaves a mark.
CHINESE PROVERB

Often and often afterwards, the beloved aunt would ask me why I had never told anyone how I was being treated. Children tell little more than animals, for what comes to them they accept as eternally established.

RUDYARD KIPLING

TO SHOW A CHILD WHAT ONCE DELIGHTED YOU, TO FIND THE CHILD'S DELIGHT ADDED TO YOUR OWN— THIS IS HAPPINESS.

J. B. PRIESTLEY

That energy which makes a child hard to manage is the energy which afterwards makes him a manager of life.

HENRY WARD BEECHER

Youth is a perpetual intoxication;
it is a fever of the mind.
FRANÇOIS DE LA ROCHEFOUCAULD

BY THE TIME A MAN REALIZES
THAT MAYBE HIS FATHER
WAS RIGHT, HE USUALLY
HAS A SON WHO THINKS
HE'S WRONG.
CHARLES WADSWORTH

Children have neither past nor
future; they enjoy the present.
JEAN DE LA BRUYÈRE

A father is the hands
that hold you safe.
AUTHOR UNKNOWN

What is a home without children? Quiet.

HENNY YOUNGMAN

CHILDREN'S TALENT TO ENDURE STEMS FROM THEIR IGNORANCE OF ALTERNATIVES.

MAYA ANGELOU

We don't stop playing because we grow old; we grow old because we stop playing.

GEORGE BERNARD SHAW

The invention of the teenager was a mistake. Once you identify a period of life in which people get to stay out late but don't have to pay taxes— naturally, no one wants to live any other way.

JUDITH MARTIN

4 years: My daddy can do anything!
7 years: My dad knows a lot. . .
    a whole lot.
8 years: My father does
    not know quite everything.
12 years: Oh well, naturally,
    Father does not know that either.
14 years: Oh, Father? He is
    hopelessly old-fashioned.
21 years: Oh, that man—he
    is out of date!
25 years: He knows a
    little bit about it, but not much.
30 years: I must find
    out what Dad thinks about it.
35 years: Before we decide,
    we will get Dad's idea first.
50 years: What would Dad have
    thought about that?
60 years: My dad
    knew literally everything!
65 years: I wish I could
    talk it over with Dad once more.

ANONYMOUS

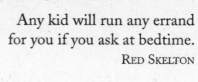

Any kid will run any errand
for you if you ask at bedtime.
RED SKELTON

PRETTY MUCH ALL THE
HONEST TRUTH-TELLING
THERE IS IN THE WORLD IS
DONE BY CHILDREN.
OLIVER WENDELL HOLMES

Our greatest natural resource is
the minds of our children.
WALT DISNEY

Kids: They dance before they learn
there is anything that isn't music.
WILLIAM STAFFORD

It is not easy to be crafty and winsome at the same time, and few accomplish it after the age of six.
JOHN W. GARDNER AND
FRANCESCA GARDNER REESE

If children are to keep alive their inborn sense of wonder, they need the companionship of at least one adult who can share it, rediscovering with them the joy, excitement, and mystery of the world we live in.
RACHEL CARSON

EACH DAY OF OUR LIVES, WE MAKE DEPOSITS IN THE MEMORY BANKS OF OUR CHILDREN.
CHARLES R. SWINDOLL

Can't you see the Creator of the universe, who understands every secret, every mystery, sitting patiently and listening to a four-year-old talk to Him? That's a beautiful image of a father.
JAMES DOBSON

FOR A NEW TAKE ON GOD'S KINGDOM, SPEND TIME WITH A CHILD TODAY.
PAMELA MCQUADE

Someday you will know that a father is much happier in his children's happiness than in his own. I cannot explain it to you: It is a feeling in your body that spreads gladness through you.
HONORÉ DE BALZAC

Sometimes the grace of God appears wonderfully in young children.
MATTHEW HENRY

A three-year-old child is a being who gets almost as much fun out of a fifty-six-dollar set of swings as he does out of finding a small green worm.
BILL VAUGHAN

CHILDREN NEED LOVE, ESPECIALLY WHEN THEY DO NOT DESERVE IT.
HAROLD HULBERT

A characteristic of the normal child is he doesn't act that way very often.
AUTHOR UNKNOWN

There are not seven wonders of the world in the eyes of a child. There are seven million.
WALT STREIGHTIFF

IF YOUR CHILDREN LOOK
UP TO YOU, YOU'VE MADE A
SUCCESS OF LIFE'S BIGGEST JOB.
AUTHOR UNKNOWN

If I had my child to raise
all over again,
I'd build self-esteem first
and the house later.
I'd fingerpaint more
and point the finger less.
I would do less correcting
and more connecting.
I'd take my eyes off my watch,
and watch with my eyes.
I'd take more hikes
and fly more kites.
I'd stop playing serious—
and seriously play.
I would run through more fields
and gaze at more stars.
I'd do more hugging
and less tugging.
DIANE LOOMANS

THE LIGHTER SIDE

The one thing children wear out
faster than shoes is parents.
JOHN J. PLOMP

CHILDREN SELDOM MISQUOTE
YOU. IN FACT, THEY USUALLY
REPEAT WORD FOR WORD
WHAT YOU SHOULDN'T
HAVE SAID.
AUTHOR UNKNOWN

Children are a lot like wet cement.
Whatever falls on them
makes an impression.
HAIM GINOTT

Mother Nature is wonderful.
Children get too old for piggyback
rides just about the same time
they get too heavy for them.
AUTHOR UNKNOWN

If you want to recapture your youth,
just cut off his allowance.
AL BERNSTEIN

WHEN BUYING A USED CAR,
PUNCH THE BUTTONS ON THE
RADIO. IF ALL THE STATIONS
ARE ROCK AND ROLL, THERE'S
A GOOD CHANCE THE
TRANSMISSION IS SHOT.
LARRY LUJACK

When I was a boy of fourteen, my
father was so ignorant I could hardly
stand to have the old man around. But
when I got to be twenty-one, I was
astonished at how much the old man
had learned in seven years.
MARK TWAIN

You know you're a dad
when you say things like. . .
"You didn't beat me. I let you win!"

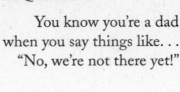

You know you're a dad
when you say things like. . .
"No, we're not there yet!"

YOU KNOW YOU'RE A
DAD WHEN YOU SAY
THINGS LIKE. . .
"EAT IT! IT WILL GROW HAIR
ON YOUR CHEST."

You know you're a dad
when you say things like. . .
"Turn off those lights. Do you think
I'm made of money?"

Ask your child what he wants for
dinner only if he's buying.
FRAN LEBOWITZ

If the new American father feels bewildered and even defeated, let him take comfort from the fact that whatever he does in any fathering situation has a 50 percent chance of being right.

BILL COSBY

TAKE HEART! YOUR CONSISTENT, LOVING DISCIPLINE WILL ULTIMATELY TEACH YOUR CHILDREN TO DISCIPLINE THEMSELVES. THEN YOUR JOB WILL BE EASIER.

BRUCE BICKEL AND STAN JANTZ

Never lend your car to anyone to whom you have given birth.

ERMA BOMBECK

I have found that the best way
to give advice to your children is
to find out what they want
and then advise them to do it.
HARRY S. TRUMAN

YOU KNOW CHILDREN ARE
GROWING UP WHEN THEY
START ASKING QUESTIONS
THAT HAVE ANSWERS.
JOHN J. PLOMP

Daughters are like flowers:
They fill the world with beauty
and sometimes attract pests.
AUTHOR UNKNOWN

There are times when parenthood
seems nothing more than feeding
the hand that bites you.
PETER DE VRIES

I love to play hide-
and-seek with my kid,
but some days, my goal is to find a
hiding place where he can't find me
until after high school.
AUTHOR UNKNOWN

WHEN CHARLES FIRST SAW
OUR CHILD MARY, HE SAID
ALL THE PROPER THINGS FOR
A NEW FATHER. HE LOOKED
UPON THE POOR LITTLE RED
THING AND BLURTED, "SHE'S
MORE BEAUTIFUL THAN THE
BROOKLYN BRIDGE."
HELEN HAYES

Many a man wishes he were
strong enough to tear a telephone
book in half—especially if he
has a teenage daughter.
GUY LOMBARDO

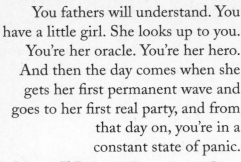

You fathers will understand. You have a little girl. She looks up to you. You're her oracle. You're her hero. And then the day comes when she gets her first permanent wave and goes to her first real party, and from that day on, you're in a constant state of panic.

STANLEY T. BANKS IN *FATHER OF THE BRIDE*

A LITTLE GIRL IS SUGAR AND SPICE AND EVERYTHING NICE—ESPECIALLY WHEN SHE'S TAKING A NAP.

AUTHOR UNKNOWN

Hot dogs always seem better out than at home, so do french-fried potatoes, so do your children.

MIGNON MCLAUGHLIN

Labor Day is a glorious holiday because your child will be going back to school the next day. It would have been called Independence Day, but that name was already taken.
BILL DODD

WATCHING YOUR DAUGHTER BEING COLLECTED BY HER DATE FEELS LIKE HANDING OVER A MILLION-DOLLAR STRADIVARIUS TO A GORILLA.
JIM BISHOP

The father of a daughter is nothing but a high-class hostage. . . . When his daughter puts her arm over his shoulder and says, "Daddy, I need to ask you something," he is a pat of butter in a hot frying pan.
GARRISON KEILLOR

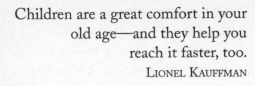

Children are a great comfort in your old age—and they help you reach it faster, too.

LIONEL KAUFFMAN

WHEN MY KIDS BECOME WILD AND UNRULY, I USE A NICE, SAFE PLAYPEN. WHEN THEY'RE FINISHED, I CLIMB OUT.

ERMA BOMBECK

On how to diaper a baby: Spread the diaper in the position of the diamond with you at bat. Then fold second base down to home and set the baby on the pitcher's mound. Put first base and third together, bring up home plate, and pin the three together. Of course, in case of rain, you gotta call the game and start all over again.

JIMMY PIERSALL

A child enters your home and for the next twenty years makes so much noise you can hardly stand it. The child departs, leaving the house so silent you think you are going mad.
JOHN ANDREW HOLMES

ONE OF LIFE'S GREATEST MYSTERIES IS HOW THE BOY WHO WASN'T GOOD ENOUGH TO MARRY YOUR DAUGHTER CAN BE THE FATHER OF THE SMARTEST GRANDCHILD IN THE WORLD.
JEWISH PROVERB

A man finds out what is meant by a spitting image when he tries to feed cereal to his infant.
AUTHOR UNKNOWN

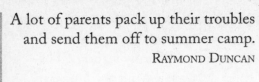

A lot of parents pack up their troubles
and send them off to summer camp.
RAYMOND DUNCAN

THE DIFFICULT THING
ABOUT CHILDREN IS THAT
THEY COME WITH NO
INSTRUCTIONS. YOU PRETTY
WELL HAVE TO ASSEMBLE
THEM ON YOUR OWN.
JAMES DOBSON

My father used to play with my
brother and me in the yard.
Mother would come out and say,
"You're tearing up the grass."
"We're not raising grass," Dad
would reply. "We're raising boys."
HARMON KILLEBREW